ABOUT THE AUTHOR

When Kyile was a child growing up his role models were authors like Alfred Lawrence, Roald Dahl, Mark Twain. Kyile is studying for a Bachelor's creative writing degree at Brunel University.

Living in UK, born and raised, Kyile has seen the open world, loves socialising, meeting people from different social integral society relationships.

Hiyaku's words of inspiration are: *Don't give up and don't frown upon reality because reality will never leave you behind, it's unto you. It has nothing to do with being materialistic, being materialistic it's more pessimistic than a bowl of Cheerios.*

Kyile managed to publish his first contemporary fictional fantasy short novel which is 125 pages long. He could not have done this without the studies into his own self-awareness and the human psychology of thought process.

With the support of his publishing agency, Author House, Kyile wrote his first book, which he named *The Tenrux Society*, which he concedes as captivated talent. Kyile began his adventures morally from studying reading books and writing, while learning about his favourite subject, astronomy.

Unlike his father who is a musician, Kyile decided to progress his life in the role model of his own choice, becoming a writer.

Kyile Jacquin Carter

THE POEM POAM MOEM MOAM BOOK

AUSTIN MACAULEY PUBLISHERS™

LONDON • CAMBRIDGE • NEW YORK • SHARJAH

A CIP catalogue record for this title is available from the British Library.

ISBN 9781398464155 (Paperback)
ISBN 9781398464162 (ePub e-book)

www.austinmacauley.com

First Published 2023
Austin Macauley Publishers Ltd ®
1 Canada Square
Canary Wharf
London
E14 5AA

POEMS

Life line

(List Poem)

The binge from alcohol.

The clash from gastronomy.

My specs are for saving money.

My telescopes for visiting clouds.

One eyed cocker for a patch.

I have no ship.

I'm no pirate.

The blackness of my sheep.

The whiteness of my teeth.

I'm smiling all the time.

I'm rhyming with my smile.

My whispers are golden.

My feet are cheesy.

My rocket has no gasoline.

My ship had no sales.

My pocket has holes.

Which leaves me totally broke.

And on my knees.

Heart ♡
(Love poem (Aubade))

The measles,

I looked into the mirror once,

I awoke out of bed looked down onto the sun,

the nail,

I stepped onto seeped,

right into my toe,

right threw the other side into my toenail.

Whilst the bed blankets hung onto me,

I held,

Tightly onto the ground.

The rained beneath me,

I began to shake to haze from ground to ceiling,

red rain painted before the sky was blue,

I lost my voice,

I lost my mind,

my vision,

the sunrise can see me though I cannot see it.

I'm blind,

white seagulls flying around searching for chips on the floor,

I danced in vain I lay beside a turtle on the beach,

your green skin hard shell made me quiver inside the sheets which had
shaped itself into my body,

while I lay besides,

the blue sky lit up with green crocs,

I feel your shave closing shaving slowly rising up and down my body,

teeth chattering from above the foam of blood.

Life lingers from beneath me,

like living inside a shell tough, as mussels,

I reach for my beach towel to keep dry lying there in blood pool of pain,

I feel the sun would never go down again,

your heat is painfully a joyful cuss,

suspicious mind of rhythmic rhythm,

the cupboards walked alone around my house.

The Calling of a Witch
(Colloquial Poem)

Wat me ah she dat,

Mi si dis ya wicked woman,

Ah she deh behind dah tree,

Ah mi she ah hide from,

Ah mi she ah cry fah,

She ah cry she ah cry,

Mi ah look pon she,

Mi ah wondah ah wah she ah cry fah,

Ah she "diss ya" olda woman ah she,

Ah di white witch "diss ya" ah wicked woman dat fi bombocklaat.

Wah she ah ball fah,

Mi nah go no weh

Near she she deh deh ah stink she ah witch fi bloodclaat,

Ah stink like sour puss,

We ah run from deya run run run from dis tree,

Mi si dis ya witch in another life time she still looks dah fuking same.

How did the devil consume me

(Visual Poem: 'The Ring around the Roses')

The ring around the roses.

A cup full of daisies.

A tissu, A tissu, we

All fell down.

The ring around the roses,

A tray full of

muffins, sunflowers, petals,

and pumpkin seeds.

How did the Devil consume

Me? With, Vanilla pods in

Pink, champagne. After eights, and

dinner dates, once addiction kicked in

with a stroke from an overdose of tastefulness.

The ring around the, roses.

A cup full of doses.

A tissu, A tissu, I fell down.

Erasure Poem

Now rejoice has you with such evil, far north of, London.

Upon my cheeks, braces my pole.

Luxury preferred to glory,

However wealth placed onto,

my path,

Oh, voice answer me now,

Rejoice my crown,

Answer my courage fluctuate my spirit,

Hopes I will demand with all my fortitude,

To lose my life dancing around,

A post,

I shall depart,

My intention be done by pain,

Not by love by sacrifices,

Ah dear sister,

I must fell,

Or never must heaven save me that farewell,

again.

The blood of my night

Death in the fire of light,

Demons crawl amongst men like swords,

Hale my king's name solstice solitude,

Mere mirror of my reflection is a path for victory,

Heaven knows me,

I asked no favour,

I asked no favour my father my god,

My father lays here beneath me dead in my arms,

Oh, vanity god of light you will die,

As my life falls in on me,

As the lightened sky pales from above,

The poisoned charm within me lives,

Hale the sky's of, Uranus.

My sword fears no charm,

The tenacity of my love fears no one.

The Hidden Poet Inside The Candle, Speaks Many Voices

(Free-style Narrative Poem)

Papa poet, the many voices within himself trapped inside the fire light of a candle,

bounded by this golden vatic piece of metal chandelier,

the creamy golden chassis within the silo wet of this boneless mind glowing flame echoing my voice around the air whilst trapped inside this silhouette soulless of skinned darkness.

The whiter wax for his skin darkest ever wick swallowing his voice whilst many other voices decent into thickening centre lining of the candle. Kept wondering along an enchanted,

Cotton eyed centre lining which burns away to a winding down sealed cove which is connected to this shiny silver chandelier withering to the séance of dance slowly disintegrating inside the centre ear piece,

Until I believe I'm fully deaf to no longer hear the footsteps of dance to this peacefulness thy wither to in vain.

Living in pain the rest of my life in a day on the edge of a desk centred in the middle,

Of an empty loft.

No window,

No sound,

Nothing entered nothing cost,

Not even the whistles could be heard from a throne,

No air no sound no feet no mouth mumbles,

Not even solstice of the wind that blows from the world outside of the living.

Living a life inside the darkness with nothing more than myself papa poet drawing with the fire and light which is reflecting the corridors of an empty shallow desk,

where I wanted to be free,

I could not breathe,

I could not get out,

I wanted to leapt out and feel the free world outside from these locked doors from inside the candle wax of many voices,

I wither inside the metal enchanted vatic chandelier.

Living the life on the edge, waiting for something to happen,

In a day or a night where nothing would be suddenly.

The light would come soon,

the fire would not rise now or then,

A voice would have spoken back to me like,

I was the god of fire.

Was there a hope,

was there a sign of bark and soil,

Or feeling maybe a feeling for the living had its simple unjust unrest whilst life living on the edge of a desk,

the question had not been answered or not.

It has to be said the colour of your skin make me frightened so frightened,

That I couldn't move a single muscle nor sole.

The voice of my sole entirely has been given the chanted light to breathe again,

With inside this emptiness from with inside the darkness from with inside the light from with inside my mind and sole which has forbiddingly started to cove down into the candle wick deep deeper inside the light,

I seem the mindlessly,

I start to sear across the darkness,

within the empty mess of space,

Like I,

Could feel myself again.

This is the day of when,

Papa poet's dream had begun.

The heated candle started to burn so slowly underneath his creamy skin
surrounded by this golden vatic piece of metal chandelier,

The creamy golden chassis within the silo wet of this boneless minded less
glowing around the darkness of,

this soulless skin.

The reflection heated,

This moment of intensity from the very first strike of the matchstick,

Whom would have lightened the thought from where the light began,

Which was only driven by curiosity of mind.

The mind-blowing curiosity of arithmetic,

My vision started to blur this wrinkled wretched large nose piece,

Nose and large lips,

The cold glass in the mirror began to mummer with the stream of heat which
fortified me

me from every moment of living,

The light of each every sentence pouring downside the burning edge of the
candles wax, Paws reflecting the light then retracting the darkness.

No more eyes for vision, just heat

pure heat and juice from the air coming out of his mouth piece

glowingly disintegrating inside the flame,

The light shone now viciously reflecting the very fore edges of this cold
enchanted room.

The breathless saint of the,

London eye which bloomed,

I could see threw the fire of memories now,

which had shone from the light then into the moon,

my mind, it is a traitorous sight,

like cream at the end of a spoon.

I papa poet hated heights but would always choose to follow the big wheel from
beneath the heartless ground below. Just from looking above the light of this
shiny spoon sitting on the edge of a desk in an empty room.

Ice of all ages

(Rondeau: Performance poem)

Icy like a dog,

barks like a forceful thrown snowball,

running through the winds hurts me like

a tree being chopped down in vain,

tails waggling like a rainbow,

frosty bites like a bee,

a spiral from the oceans,

the icy bitterness of the cold is not my friend neither is the sea,

my teeth chattering away wasn't for pleasure,

I'm frozen to the teeth,

bones of bitterness,

dinosaurs at the museum.

Emphasis

Poetry is, the rhythmical, creation to capture the essence of cord, struck by the poet, he, or she, to capture the reader's attention.

Everyone's A Prey
(Single sentence poem)

Margarita chopped peas parsley ham and, eggs,

runny lava crawling over my head,

centipede looking down into my bed,

dangling like a upside-down.

Mushrooms without legs,

pitch bends from ah synthesizer,

the howling begins to prowl me into ah solace of silence,

the windows locked out smog,

the year of droplets inside of the rain makes a puddle for a homeless frog to swim inside of.

I feel his not forget me,

not while forget me not dust camouflaged my skin,

hoping, the parrot would not see him threw the dots patched onto his skins,

the parrot eats,

maggots 'creaks cringe whilst echoing winds full of bees,

swarming near a tree they'll have you at your very own hide,

like a tear drop given,

from the rain, for a toad to hide in.

Beagle eyed reapers in the winds,

howling's rushing through the trees,

feathered choke hold a beak sitting upon my shoulder,

--dribble drabble from my beak,

you're all gobbled up nothings more to croak whilst your,

Adam's apple is currently circling around inside of my beak,

the howling never stops,

I begin to prowl myself into the distant solace silence of my croak.

Just gone too far away, memory's best friends left behind

Laughter from bowls. Doughnuts on the run. Earing's crows should wear.

Happy smiles of silence. Milking the cow. Walking the device. Hurrying home from school. Sweetheart inside the sweetshop. Golden chocolate bunnies. Watermelon.

Blackjacks. Fruit salad. A handful down my pants. Running from the barking mad dog.

Something went wrong. The dog had bitten almost too much more than he could chew.

Children of the corn. Or, like, silence of the lambs. All day playing at arcades with one twenty pence coin. Laughter at my feet. I was shy. She wasn't sweet rainbow chard. Frozen toes tingles underneath blankets. Stars fade away. Fridge door opens. Many more dance.

Giggle's parade. Face paint. Kinder eggs. Beer bottle I, love the taste of. Dry cigarettes ash on the tip, of your tongue.

I remember correctly you, was there alone with my first crush. And I, was with yours. Tables were twisted around. Like, Mars had been on the other face of, the opposite side of the moon. I wished; I was all yours. She was just too shy for you. I had wet dreams, being alone at night. You were the only one for me. As time goes by. I knew if, I saw again. I'll always be fond. Sheep's skins and, tears. The happiness inside your smile. Your, rosy glazed red cheeky cheeks. Your round, chubby arse was meant to be mine. You didn't, know my feelings. I was just young and shy at the time.

Nothing much has changed. Except, I've forgotten about your smile. I remember being given, my first chopsticks from an, Chinese takeaway. I smiled and walked away. Sat down eagerly waiting, for your help. You handed me heart burn, burps. I fell in love with. I ate it all up at home. Stains on my shirt. Crying on my way home. Having to hide you away. Talking to you on the phone. Racism, was an issue, at the time.

You were snobby and ambitious. But super cute. Which always, left me feeling, fuzzy dizzy and fizzy. You never looked at me. You blanked me totally. I spent months remembering my birthdays without you. We met at, the ice-skating rink. Our very first sight. My vision was locked. I fell over. You picked me up with your smile. I was taken far away from the scene. Dancing in the country side. The coconut clubs. Extreme measures, to stitch mend a broken heart. At least you were there for me. At least you noticed. That's what best friends were for. Looking out for each other. We danced, the night away on stage. So many ladies in town.

But none of them were mine. I forgot about her being in my mind. I started watching yours. I wished she was mine. While you were under the bedsheets with her. I was mad with jealously. Out of my mind. Just gone too far away. Memory's best friends leave behind.

Cocktails, Locked down and smoking barrels

Locked down & making memories with a slosh endless memetic indulge endure embrace every moment of my heart beat racing towards the end of the day for an outwards burst of laugher while the night owl

hoots away on his selfless puff belly one eyed blink he winks away on a perch to the day we stumble upon joy of another day once again the pain of a migraine from last night's hoot from a swig of thee older, Gin and pumpkin root. Parlay the wave hankering joy of pain thee awaking sun wrenches my eyes with a rub off my hands I stand up to close the curtains tight and shut the window from being shut, shut up I don't need all this noise in vain I've only just woken up again its 6 am in the morning what the hell is going on with all this hooting in the day there's no traffic no cars in sight fore seeing a human being would be such a delight to foresee or hear the chattering from the streets, but all I could hear is the wind air along with the hooting's of an owl, birds in my ears.

(Mixology Cocktails) 🍸 Locked down 2020 April 23rd.

The Corollavoid-19, Cocktail special. 🍸

Life style

Life is a question, not for best friends not for your dog

life is not a job, life is no different than a jog.

Life Is no different to

shouting out, I need a doctor. Life is a question, Life is not

a job. Life ain't enough to keep me from drinking beer. Life ain't enough
to keep me from without having fear.

Life is a question life is not a job, life is no different to having a problem
with the mob. Your life in a dictatorship.

Are you having your own right of way, the expression is decent ethnicity
will almost always certainly give you away.

Specially if your black, beneath the colour of your skin. The boys in blue
will certainly come for you to commit sin. Which they will more than
likely stop you in the street, because they have the light, they will asked
questions about why your aren't so bright.

Asked for the time, where have you been.

Do you know why we stopped you, it's because you were outside during
this time of day, life is a question life is not a job.

Life is what you make of it, even if you never had a job.

You will take control of your own decisions.

You will be centred by your own mistakes.

But who will depend upon your destiny to reward you with your fate.
Your final destination

The world is at stake. The question is not life, its what you have to stake.

Today is an image of tomorrow

Life's in an image, I stare upon a tree in the garden

the squares in the windows pane, a burp for my pardon.

I dreamt tomorrow will never be the same frame again and again,

As I stand still to take a picture of my birds feeding sorrowfully.

I lay my eyes upon there beneath the tree, my dog lying still inside the kennel surrounded by

a pack of bees. The hearts in a cage, I wonder why I feel so helplessly afraid and in a rage.

I wonder when my other half will finish work. Your feet are nowhere to be found my dear,

I feel I'm looking at you now. Again, and again just like yesterday same bloody shit just like today,

The parrot is still talking to himself

"Croak who's, A pretty birdy, Croak".

Same bloody shit, And I'm still thinking about why the cat never come back home.

Your feet are nowhere to be found my dear, My husband, never came home too. I answered the phone in the morning, He's not coming home the hospital said he's practically dead undergoing surgery for his head, the cat was beside him weeping on his chest and wouldn't go away

from his surgical bed, oh the piece of bad news has ruined my day.

My daughter's at school, My dinner's

on the phone. The bills came through

the door. I wish I never was at home,

The phone rang with bad news of my husband in a morg.

I needed to get out of this image of today is tomorrow,

Why should I follow tomorrow's is another day, different from now.

I feel almost still like a ghost, feeling the haunted pleasure of my heart beating outside of my chest.

I better not the pleasure of what can happen next, which will never be different than you already know.

A Sting Ray's Tail

Can

You

Find it

Far above

High and wide

Above the clouds

Like a tooth fairy above

The clouds, like cotton from

A bull, like a dog rolling over and,

Over again. A shimmering sight of an

White delight, joyfully with hot chocolate

, under a tree. Whispers of the wind residing

Around me, am I the sacred scare crow beneath

the crow upon my arm. What a wonderful sand

of whispers chirping around me. So now its

time to laugh so now it's time to cry so

now it's time to goth so now it's time

to hide so now it's time to hatch

So now it's time to die

So now it's time to

Look up again

High above

The

Sky, Now when you look up what do you see, a very friendly face deep beneath
the sea

Love dives beyond doubt

I've never been forgotten love dives beyond doubt.

Spoil them with youth forever, For forever Lasting friendship.

While they clay in the mud house, playing in the dough with rolling pins.

There jumping on the ground up and down, the whole house is in a mess.

whilst love dives beyond doubt, seamlessly they remind me of them packets of

jumping jelly beans being thrown jumping around about the roundabout,

getting me a bit out of wind.

Whilst Love dives beyond doubt, the doors

thrust open from the oven of the cooker bakes a pie risen thoroughly

to perfection seamlessly without a broken crust, or a burnt rim.

Whilst love dives beyond doubt, the sad birds sing a song of praises in the mornings.

The, joyfully essences towards the oddness of sleep brings the awakening by a noise.

A noise, that made me think it's time sleep to break a dawn.

To clean a toy room filled with a mess from frog's spawn of jelly beans and

children's play dough with rolling pins stuck on the floor, on the door on the ceiling not

forgetting on my best dress. No time for a mouth of yawns, no time to puddle

let's clear up all. All this mess of play dough jelly beans and puddles, whilst love dives

beyond doubt. Beyond doubt for nothing means less let me not awaken

again, while I'm dreaming of my day job.

Love dives beyond doubt, whilst I must rest my heart mind and soul.

Love dives beyond doubt, whilst I lean towards the trinket which fell down

In the sofas from my necklace. Love dives beyond doubt, My hands full with cotton marsh mallows from a hot chocolate cup with a diamond soul, pearls for a slice of chocolate

swiss roll. How delightful is your love, whilst love dives beyond doubt.

Crickets' Appetites 🦗

I eat crickets hum hum, yum yummy.

While lying in the grasses of melting touches,

Crickets tickle like crunchy twigs, which tickle down

my lungs in the rain. The bitter nutty aftertaste, tasted

like forests fires frost, while I lay upon a hay stack.

I could see a tractor in the mist, I leaps up from this heap

of hay, hey I say I started waving ahoy.

I leaped and jumped without watching,

The tiny cricket in my hand. I leaped

I jumped without watching those beady eyes in pain,

I felt the smidgen in my hand. The peace keeps sole less cricket

I tried to find in my hand was not a butterfly, it was a dead cricket in my hand.

While, the burden of silk tails winds in the darkness that grew behind me.

For more my tummy aches for more,

For more my tummy aches, While the greyness skies filed

with epiphany fulfilling each and every time moment of every space in the clouds.

The truths beyond the doors of heaven, my homes just not too far away now.

I'm running to the doors of heaven running towards, The awakening irony of the mores.

Helplessly wondering why, I could see my reflection from in the water. Wondering for whose jaws will become my taken apatite.

I eat crickets, hum yum, yum yummy.   While lying in the grasses of melting touches. Cricket tickle like crunchy twigs going down my tummy, slightly slurping slushily lightly like figs. The rain frosted upon my feet, I scurried around for another cricket, heap leap here we begin.

I started jumping without leaps, eating crickets gave me the joy.

So, I began to Leap heap jump without leaps watching those beady eyes in pain.

Without light without darkness, I see my cricket perish without light without darkness.

I see my tiny cricket's peace keep, the cricket's soul I tried to heap was not a treat neither was it a butterfly.

I awaken while the burden of silk tails winds after the mores, inside the darkness for more my tummy

aches for more. The darkness came for more greyness in the skies for each and every space in time the,

clouds filled with epiphany. I run beyond the awakening irony of the mores, my tears mores the awakening of myself from

outside of the moonlight sky's which shred out the light like silk. Towards the light in the distance, I

run further into the darkness outside without sight.

I followed the first steps of blindness without destiny in my sight.

The Smell

The Smell reminds me of roses, the sink had lime scale on the taps, the thorns glistened in rain droplets of Ash and flames. The carriage of a train the pain in a window frame, upon the gush of breath. I' exhale the Smell of an armpit, to hell is a shame the fire in the rain is now dripping on my face. There be the wild darkness, beyond treasure the tea of, fortune hope of the sunflower petal hope of the prey of man the birds will wither inside the pan for dusk till joy comes epiphany the next eclipse harpooning its moons. Keep the light from day to night look at the stars how they shine bright can you see me now like a butter cookie marshmallow on the fire here. there I wait for the world to desire the equation of life within self. Destiny makes you and me feel and think of love, The passionate passing over the mud pigs will play eat and shit the Smell of shit reminds me of what I used to do with it. Make time to associate our minds because four is better than honey and more is better than money the Smell of a dollar bill or the smell of a eagles kill to prey for money to prey for food is it all the same the same stinking mood from. Far to near we prioritize in distance lengthy time it takes to become one's persistent. Miraculous enough there isn't enough fortune in every single day's because once it's done the light goes away. We say everyone happy, but why is there poverty the Smell of tramps of rats and novelty, the price to pay for such a kindred spirit we walk away from the smell of indignity. Perhaps the life we follow must be a gun and tonic of the tide waves of the metaphoric distortion

Games train automobiles and planes trains what do we do now, don't you think the smells still the same. Just a different setting for the night for you to do a shit. A king a Smell now go smell your armpit. The cold sense of aroma, crow with thunder and bolts together like an evil hunter but it's nothing mere than a shadow hunter from forest to tree, the hives already spoken bees aroma makes a splendid duel for a coma. From. Ashes to ashes dust to dust when the cat comes home you feed the bust, the dog barks the birds Hum, the insects chime, and the fruits make wine the Smell of vines grapes apes chimps Dogs frogs have you ever smelt God, I guess, not fear what you smell because if it ever could tell your smell you'd be sure be sent to hell so live a life with the smell.

A Sting Ray's Tail

(Single Sentence Visual Poem)

Can

you

find, it

far above

high and wide

above, the clouds,

the tooth fairy from above,

the clouds like cotton candy,

the bull, the dog rolling over and,

over again. The shimmering sight of an

white delight, joyful with a hot chocolate

sitting under the tree, whispers of the wind

residing around me, am I the sacred scare crow beneath

the crow upon my arm, What a wonderful sand

of whispers chirping around the farm, so now

it's time to laugh, so now it's time to cry, so

now it's time to smile, so now it's time

to hide, so now it's time to hatch,

so now it's time to die,

So now it's time to

Look, up again

high above

the

sea.

Now when you look up what do you see, a very friendly face deep beneath the sea.

Fate of your own decisions

NoooOoooooooOoNoooOoooooooOooooooooo, how dare this become an inseparable fate, A diseases that's stung an inseparable fame. Now we can't even sneeze or breath in the breeze. The shame of hearing a sneeze 🤧 it's like looking over your shoulder in the morning with a mouse nibbling on your forehead for a bit of cheese. But you were too sick 🤒 and tied to even move an Inch in any direction from left to right or even nobble a knee to even make the finch to flick that cheese away from your forehead.

Too bad for the lost, in a sake of the wake from the coronavirus, which has buried our heads in shame. We walk in fear of having our lives taken away from the very same shame of fate from our livelihoods. No more school 🏫 for us which is a crying shame for all of us.

Can't wait for the day, I remember this day like it was almost forgotten fate,

The unethically order of

fate begins to unravel

inside an unmisable dialogue within earth.

The official sin

Fright night had begun, I'm the official of my sleigh, the penguins in the corridors of heaven.

I have not woken up yet, bang clunk bank. Action has its flank, naturally people die my heart sank, I sink like a broken rotary arm how ever did I die, the trip kept me awake last night while i Kept tossing and turning watching every clunk, vases not faces, it was already past the hour. Two bid flap why you got to be sour. The cracked thing on the screen, the blossoming bloom of this song, however does one say the mole who dug his whole had his way. Treasure not treaty, I circle like a sweaty packed in a bag. Ready to bowl Like my bland packed salad roll trapped in a bowl, how do I meant fate when I'm about to land six feet under, the crate melt. The possum of life had finally begun not only, Glacier's mumble.

The night was very young, a pale faced lung, a woman, a man just had the same fuming song, burning up in the atmosphere, like lime, the smell of porridge and canola limes, chimes dimes. Where are we going to land, death becomes her before, I make the demand.

Fright night is the fusion of this hickory hickory, dock tick tock tick tock the clock. "What time is it, it's time we got to go leave our bodies from behind creeping out of solitude

silence and lust the love game was never in a rush.

Let's hope the green of Mars never had any rust, the green edges of Mars the green chocolate bars, the edges of the moon the rover to return home soon. These edges never game just humble and pie. Do not ever take the edge piece because it will be desired by spoons knives and forks, those edges are rather blunt, are we scared of texture and tastes before the cry's, the edges aren't copping up to it mark my wife was pregnant, how dare they make it crash, from high edge to low edge the pressures almost up, however. Do I fear the floor those edges aren't even bent, more softly than ever. I wish could make the bed, the smell of life gushing by per second, if I wasn't on edge, I'd meet very well marvel

Legends and unfold time in a different way. The flash of a man the edge of time has been broken. If I was a flash, the edge would not be broken. The field of joy was full of grass, the

wind was only what was broken, A dying race for

Faculty, do we need to stare, this book was a sin to read, we both died, we hit the edge of the cliff in a

Chopper edge, fledge fall out. Instead, we jumped before letting the edges take us all out.

Me Too movement

Within the next horizon was a founded day, three days away from the day of diversity and

order

The law remains the same people are generically gentle with emotions towards each other.

The night was young a pale, grace in porridge with some sediment of mood to enhance its contagiousness and deep pit of sludge, the smell of canola vanilla remains. A smell of a bought posing standing and staring in my face smiling prejudicially in the light and dark

MOMENTS, while I swallowed the first mouth fall of salt then tequila. I opened my mouth

and swallowed hard

My eyes for blood orange juice, my stance for courage in my skin tight trousers rolling over

my buttocks.

Round and cheesy with a little croup crease for cream. I loved the days where I could run wild like being naked in the stars that shined down from above the sound system. Born this

way by Lady gaga

Gave me a forming elevation raising my manufacture, while I swayed my croup from side to side left to right vigorously in a emotional manner. I've never felt as this before being able to

come to terms with being happy and croup facing the sky dancing in my living room while

the radio sang gay.

I could feel the Sweat dropping of my dick, my chest was risen high for nothing more could stand in the way from this point on no way to turn back the memories of geisha, The red cheeked little girl being rose upon. Nothing mere to share of happiness the desperate moment

of solitude had gasped for air.

His face was the memory of my dispersed moment for ecstasy, I wanted to feel like this again the toilet rush then being left to fall in a pit of water being flushed down the big no pittance no frogs were allowed to interact or interfere with this particular situation as his approach was written in tears above my eyes, Gay independent day, please suck my dick before Thursday because today was already Friday night and yesterday was

gay independence day.

I become confused to what happened, three days ago now I'm staring at my ceiling dancing in ecstasy, I've no longer enough strength to cover life of loving no longer. "This was it, this was the very last first and foremost chance to be able to forget the fact that the world would know that it was all a mistake, I didn't know the will of mans desire was a temptation for

evil love and hatred.

I will never tell a sole the truth about the love you gave to me, the hidden world of your evil staff, your awkward and vile suggestion of dancing my memories into your own words of

dreams, like I hadn't even existed to begin with.

I can no longer live with it myself the existence of your life which ruined my very own. The world was not to know, what happened that night you took me whole.

The Gold And Silver Fish

Whose Fish is that? I know I know.

Its full of joy quite happy though.

Full of joy like a fish,

I watch the babies, I cry hello.

He gives his Fish a shake,

And laughs until her belly aches.

Then throw some powder in the bowl,

I hear the distant waves of fins and bubbles.

The Fish is Gold, Silver and deep,

the food had gone the bubbles sleep.

The cloudy parrot

The parrot, cloudy parrot bitter tail trails behind

in the distance of echoing maggots, peeping threw

the door closed tightly shut. Mirror mirrors on the

wall why is this tree full of bees swarming like a death

bed, a demons oars they'll have you knee deep in pitta blood,

chitter chatter a parrot flocking. I'm choking on a worm guzzle,

Guzzle beak of the eagle you see a crow or a toad if you've never

been alone unseen a parrot talking alone up a tree full of bees the evil

throat near its feet, chitter chatter brings me closer to that evil buzz drives

me away from so far to adrift. Away with the wind, I was gone in the wind

from my very own sins. The parrot, Oh beauty oh bees of darkness buzzing croak of death

claws of hell drink the blood of my farther, hell sings beyond the flood without water, mirror

mirrors forgive my sins of fear, hope beagles eyes reaper threw the winds. Howl's beyond, Mars who's behind you

the deafening choke hold of Jaws claws, the parrot never had teeth neither did jaws have claws. Do not turn around do not go out the door.

Sea bed
(Free verse poem)

I lay down on my bed begin to dream

the sheets were silk with satin shiny golden bream,

The fish swam around me in my mind,

the comfort from my mattress helped me find.

The place in my mind for which I lay there with my heart at rest,

Solemnly but slowly I begin to sink,

With the feelings of water sounds from splashing soles of bream.

Heart broken my eyes shut there began to weeping,

Followed by my tender slow movements from my feet.

Like,

Aladdin I yonder threw with my sheets,

in heaven wonder why my heart began to beat.

God help me if only I can make a wish, three rubs of my satin

sheets will bring me a dish, something sweet and humble like ocean pie.

No yonder Aladdin can't look me in the eyes, the pet of my sea bed looks away.

The trinkets of sea horses dance away, the sound of there songs is a maze.

To the end of the bottom of the oceans inside a maze, this is a journey to the end.

My sleepless nightmare will never come again.

myths vs the cloudy parrot

The parrot, cloudy parrot bitter tail trails behind

in the distance of echoing maggots, peeping threw

the door closed tightly shut. Mirror mirrors on the

wall why is this tree full of bees swarming like a death

bed, a demons oars they'll have you knee deep in pitta blood,

chitter chatter a parrot flocking. I'm choking on a worm guzzle,

Guzzle beak of the eagle you see a crow or a toad if you've never

been alone unseen a parrot talking alone up a tree full of bees the evil

throat near its feet, chitter chatter brings me closer to that evil buzz drives

me away from so far to adrift. Away with the wind, I was gone in the wind

from my very own sins. The parrot, Oh beauty oh bees of darkness buzzing croak of death

claws of hell drink the blood of my farther, hell sings beyond the flood without water, mirror

mirrors forgive my sins of fear, hope beagles eyes reaper threw the winds. Howl's beyond, Mars who's behind you

the deafening choke hold of Jaws claws, the parrot never had teeth neither did jaws have claws. Do not turn around do not go out the door.

The pale skin on my tits began to peel while laying there on the beach, the shallow skulls of the boat were on tidal,

It was noon, the smoke risen from the sands like a microscopic mule, the heat burns threw me like Sulphur mud sitting on my face while I bench on the wooden bed, time tick tocks away howls from the wind. My fins up in agony concerned for the sunlight above the wind, where I could see no more sea, I could see no more water the windless sails turned into a goliath demon parrot, risen above the clouds. The sea turned to dust the clouds turned to ashes, I hail onto my feet for the step onto my perch. Ashes to ashes dust to dust my feet began to turn to dust, before you known my body became to turn to ashes, like ashes to dust I turned into a parrot from the curse of the red eyed goliath de

Red Devil Sin

Red devil sin, liquor store beneath
my porch oh my oh mine bottle for
life. I lie between red devil sin, oh my
oh mine,   the bedsheets rumbles begin
to shiver while the noises of the trains
going by,   My window pane, Red devil
sin snap my wrist is now that time again,
Red devil sin of shame liquor in my veins
oh my oh mine red devil sin oh holy shame
of justice oh holy juice shame over and over
again, I feel sick of feeling ashamed oh now
trauma I feel the sip   climbing down the
ladder to put the bin outside of its misery,
The bees bliss trees wither as I look upon
my knees feeling helpless to kneel upon
a dizzying shame, I walk in shame be my
vomit be my heart beat be my emptiness
while my heart beats for nothing less than
red devil sin the liquor of my flame the shiny
red bottle sits upon my window pane again
again and over again nothing changes the red
devil sin from being there rotting in between my legs.

The spirit of my chef

I woke in the morning, I fell like sadness, "" to hell
with the summer, its open finally. My chefs awake in
the kitchen, oh my goodness there's a fox at the stove,
Mother never knew, I let the draft in last night I kept the
window open in hope, Mr fox would return. " There are leaves
everywhere in the kitchen, oh my god, what is this mess, what
am I seeing, a bloody mess in my kitchen. Mother had fainted just
before she could hurdle the brush at me. "Oh my child how
do you like your, Brussels soft or spongey. I want them to be hard,
Like frozen leaves falling from the ice clouds high above the ceiling.

It's winter, Mr fox remember, Mr fox what's your name? ""Wondrous fox. Wondrous,
You're wonderful. "hmmm, The smell of your tail makes me feel hungry. Your mother
must be a, Wondrous genius. ""Yes my mother was a hunter, My father was a mole
fox always stayed down the hole nothing less."" Conjuring popsicle, my teeth are
levitating. ""Feeling the erg again, uncontrollably "Hahaha. I want to play a game
let's see if you can find me let me hide first. ""Games I don't play games, look at
my fur, rigid and vain my tails stands firm my ears are poking up. If we play this
game, Your time will be up and I'll have to go home.

The knot of Family

Bitch arse niggas got injunctions on my arse

un shit, an still be stalking me. The knot of family

making me tired day by day, like the moon rover landing

of jfk, for the wrong or the right love is hate. The knot

of family is ah kindred shame. Dem ting deh ah nuh right

,coronavirus plague. The knot of family still be stalking

me an shit, made me think the holy bible was a curse an shit.

Bitch arse niggas mi got mi own shit, jealous arse niggas still be

talking to me in my sleep an shit, Bitch arse niggas trying to provoke mi an shit,

I ain't doing nothing though to stir this shit. Bitch arse niggas becoming

muslin an shit the knot of a family trying to turn me against Christianity

un shit, why the fuck these bitches be tripping like, the knot of family

I worked for my own shit. Ah why these bitch arse niggas be lying in shit,

for money not love be deh kindred of hate. The knot of family smoking each other
like it ah cocaine blame. Bitch arse niggas I ain't gwan do shit just wait for the clock
to tick ova fi my turn un shit.

Let it rain let it rain we all dying un shit anyway, nobody waan tek deh blame.

Without Light, Without Darkness

I see thyself perish without light
without darkness, I see my peace keep.

The soul I tried to heap was not a treat
neither a Butterfly 🦋 I awaken while the

burden of silk tails winds, I inside
the darkness for more tummy aches

for more darkness for more greyness.
Sky's with epiphany fulfilling truth,

Beyond doors I awaken the irony of tears.
Mores awakening thyself, myself from

outside of thy silk casing. I shred
out the silk towards the light, distantly

outside without sight. I followed the first

steps of blindness without destiny.

Life in an image

Life's in an image
the, windows in a
frame.

The heart's in a cage,
The dog's in a kennel.
Your feet are nowhere
to be found.

The parrot still talking to
himself "Croak who's
A pretty birdy, Croak".
The cat never came back home.

My husband, undergoing surgery,
My daughter's at school, My dinners
on the phone. The bills came through
the door.

In the end of all, the sudden incident of my,
Suicide could not ignore it all, So I was just
a fool, for thinking I could have it all for myself without there being any
complications.

Tale of tales
(Quotes POAM MOAM (shorty story))

A fairy believes Vampires exists, we have bloodlines fighting against estranged unheard of diseases. Was it the bite of first love from a Vampires depression, or a bite from a feast. We hardly understand these mysterious mystical anomaly's living within our very own worlds. But so we have a new kind of sunset a new moon with a forest of, New emerging emotions. What if curing our current situation with these new unpopular diseases, was about understanding and uncovering what's behind these new emotions that dwindle the integrity's of these new understandings within other species. We await to find a cure for coronavirus and Sars!, What if we only needed to entrap and understand how the emotions unveils itself within our very own, Emotional platform perhaps. Maybe there's another answer to something unexplainable.

The NHS

(Quotes POAM MOAM)

Bolder eagerness of heated moments awaits,

"Hager upon liquidity their thickly heated flooring.

Shine of lamination gluey addictiveness reflects satanic odds an utterly even trod,

bow your head how dirty are your shoes.

Walk the wards with eyes of steel,

maternity wards filled with,

Joyously drugs, pillows of chocolate, Rollo's coffin filled. Empty Nests dead people's eggs, cross red texts, paraffin paraphernalia , Red cross, red, Docherty pox, death precocity.

Dedication

I see myself as the premier of my Jeep

I sow my sorrow I sow my peace keep.

The sole I tried to find was not a mathematician.

To sit inside a class full of Peter Pans was not a competition because

I know it.

To be in a class full of poets magpies and toes, the buzzards sting while

the beach bum's stuck to a stool with a drool, It's now it's 2021 any fool

can be a poet, The clocks are a ticking brawl.

Time is ticking away as we came nearer to a climax, wither while the tidal of winds

Reach the Wizards of Oz's, Am I the snob if noble of proses.

What makes me feel the applause, this for more my tummy aches for more

dire beside these oars flapping around like jaws.

Inside the darkness of the greyness sky's lighten up classroom door

with an epiphany exclamation of delight fulfilling the truth beyond the mores,

of the beach the sand and coral floors which will never clap shut its jaws.

The Garbage Truck
(Poetic Storytelling)

The hidden fact is, this is not the garnish of aromas from a garbage dumpster truck.

Introduction, the garbage dumpster truck has its limits unlike you and any other person whom, "Is reading this story. The fact is, you would not usually find the things you want from a garbage dumpster truck "just smells and rotting carcasses, basically dead dreams. But heaven knows, I' didn't expect the unexpected to happen while reading this, Poetic

Short story. "Who would have thought, I'd find you all here. It looks like we're on the move again see you on the next street.

"Frankly for thought, The Smell of vines are making me ache' here we go again down Lea valley roadside in number twenty eight, how many rotten eggs and dates pilled with smog, a Murray of Ash and eighteen bottles of cog ten bottles of coke, "noise, abaft sound of flies. For 'madness I' closed the lid shut then closed my eyes, I' could see two mountains collide "crash, this is madness the floor was pale with brown ink covered with black bodies and red eyes. I' could never have seen so many dead spies before my eyes. The Smell reminds me of roses while the thorns ambush the light, "forgive me not for trying to tell you this was not going to be a pleasant ride. This is madness "argh, two men fucking in bed the things you see from a dumpster, would turn you totally upset. "number thirty, let's skip twenty nine. Instead in the rain, I' danced without an umbrella. 'Whooshing up ahead, I'd better start trotting, "shit someone's dead. On while I' hanged gliding on air, number seventy "Halt, oi hang on mate there's a monkey in ere 🙈" eek "eek 'to hell hang on there, hello little chimp, now we have a shoulder someone who could see. Number seventy one 'woohoo Nelly the elephant, this one's full of nuts, "I shouted this one full. "shouted, open your hutch number seventy three, this one full of pee , there a building up ahead full of ice lard and saturation, people and pig tails, it's 6am in the morning this doesn't explain the dead. When walking, I'm living I' should be upon my bed, for this day of stress I'm totally a red neck. We could not see the end of this fuming tail, bed mobs and broomsticks that was some fucking tale, one clever fucking lion 🦁 who never wanted to go to hell, he never wanted to eat them all, just only because he was hungry not because he was tall not because he was a fool neither because he was a lion afraid of them all. They broke the rules while I was wandering alone broken hearted, So I killed and ate them until I was farting.

'Clearing the cobwebs' exercise

- I wrote down the first line that comes into my head.

The hidden facet is, this is not the garnish of aromas from. A garbage dumpster truck.

- I wrote down a smell.

Ink

- I wrote down a visual image.

A garbage dumpster truck 🚛.

- I wrote down an emotion.

Fear, heartbroken, destiny, self-love, desire, reputation, anger.

The Tape
(Quotes POAM MOAM)

God's love for humanity on earth, what an ungodly deed was woven by the paralysis determined.

The Metaphor of self-light for the duty of which we're in search of abundance, the priority of being within love endure light begun where the heaven rows the waters of fear. Fight off the darkness then shake out the truth beyond a solicitude of justice that may come with a humming of traditional tranquillity or nothing less there other than a trace of dust beyond the aftermath. God's of Rose's a Fallen star while we cry for happiness, we get cheers for joy whenever we laughed for joy we gave fear for everyone who raged beyond anger they did not vow the rise of the sociological silence.

There was nothing mere but dividend trilogy yet once more time back in my diversity grew the Metaphor of self-light that came upon my pin lay there an empty cluster, the box of shadows within. "I would not take this red tape for justice, not only had I been awaken from the nightmare afraid of the darkness which kept my eyes open walking among the dead. Through the night on and on the footsteps rose beyond evolution. "For that I am no man of my world, their grave for my right hand lay an oak, a tree nevertheless than a boat in a sunken ship without a throat. I kept walking into the dusk of darkness until there was no man's land, for this, I could see in amputation of my self-seeking sympathy. A way threw the first night without the time or a coffee. I wondered into the aftermath of one empty field of horse shit, WTF is this? Was I meant to be forsaken a man of justice peace and Keep. While thee was no light, While thee was no day, While thee was no darkness but nothing less than misery and emptiness. "I remembered you now in the mirror of faces, I was watching you watching me in solstice of patterns in an embezzlement. How the masses of moons could reach beyond this measurement of pleasure we wait for moral peace of human transit the destiny awaits ourselves for much greater means of life than self destruction, while the desert remains sandy the spirits uphold its grass the moons of heavens circle on a circumference at an axis of mass. Rotation does this tiny cubed particle of Fusion hold the key, to the barriers that remain open unlike anything unimaginable to see or verify to any degree of certainty? The blemishes within a dotted matrix virtual in singularity, no infrared no more clarity the man's sole is no more solemnly but sole less as there is no limits towards the damage we keep. The thread threading through "ugh its calamity Satan's passage on and on we forage for air, let alone the gasp that is not their, silent the perched bird of prey is still keeping a hold of it on edge Until the very last but not least moment Until the rise of the third moon sun will rise on again.

The Red Tap Part II
(Quotes POAM MOAM)

The red tap, the device once controlled by life, itself the light shone. Shine onto thee sparkle like a rainbow. A tree it reflects the possum fruit to bare, the turn in the knife fire in the water however along the line you cross. The red tap is not something that's real because if it was you'd really be lost. Since 1842-1880 tirades emerged of opium tea cotton a rotten price to pay for 2027. Forgive my embrace of a dying world, the words was not chosen these were woven words of a caterpillar for whose silk was not chosen to weave but given by faith. Not error not beauty not loyalty but the beast was woven from within, forget not the red tape we follow. Do I hear the sands of pollution or the cry of sea worms in pain from a plastic shame 2019 and its still all the same from territories to traitor standing in the acid rain the running man is no game and its time to run so do not wear a hat because there is nothing more left to feel, within thyself. Nothing mere nothing kind, just pretend you were alive to feel the thing you wanted most. Now do not cross the line because the red tape has already been woven into your mind now the seagulls will shit onto your face but not deliberate it was just the gust of air in your face, what is recollection, what is sovereignty the question is what the hell are you going to do about it. Today is the day its time to soil and crawl out of your bowels and into the bunker but don't worry there will be better days happier days to meant, from a poppy to an assertion of cannabinoids, can you see me now sitting there under a lime tree to bare in mind the footstep of eco evolution one more step for man one more step for man kind, can you hear me now beauty and the beast time and time again the rules were broken, time and time again you'll look out the window rain check now your looking at the clocks going backwards now there just a reflection of you in the mirror looking back at you tick tock tick tock tick tock. Illuminati the change for faces, marker dice, rocks, cucumber, dildos what's going on In this bloody world, brexit, G20, third round negotiations, are you high on life now or are you just two faced. Peacefulness or religion the choice is yours, can you trust yourselves now to find it on your own. Yeah I' believe I'm in denial Satan , I eat pork not dogs who hates God should not read on just close this tiny cube of fusion and carry on with your life, because your rotting like heroine just go cut your shoulder off and cook it in the frying pan. Suck it up with BBQ sauce then call it a cure for ham jam or marmalade.

Your head's inside your hood

Nature is like your body

Nature is like a hoody,

Nature is like a condom you put over your woody

Nature is a thing of course beauty and the beast

Nature is so pure still you cannot breath,

If you can't keep up with nature,

You then can't keep up ancient history's

If you can't keep up with ancient history

then you can't keep up with nature,

If you can't keep up with nature,

Then you can't keep up with yourself,

If you can't keep up with yourself,

Then you can't keep up with ancient history,

If you can't keep up with ancient history,

Then your heads in a bloody mess as well, As well as yourself.

Don't let yourself go, Don't let nature keep on growing without you.

You are nature,

You are selfless.

Life without You

Die another day,

For a better tomorrow or is tomorrow never done

We need a new referendum, not to end the day with a gun,

We need to buy a better bullet to dissolve the certainty drug laws we have abided to.

We must find a better solution to the problem.

Without following the traits which empowerment the United States government.

Where as you see the most important point, is simply the declination of humanity, and humanities concern to conceive the controls of the governments substance. Which is not only holding back humanity it's holding humanity back in current status policymakers droopy drools. With more to want than in fact what about what is life really about. It's not about drugs embargoes from opposing thy allied, but agenda is, to this is what it will become this is what it will be, and what will we become. However while we are surrounded by it why are we flaunting in it with our own lives. Circumstantial evidence provides proof that a legalization conversation over drug policy it is a turmoil conversation which should have been abandoned decades ago. Because of its boosting superpower constancy to destroying human life which you have already seen , you can see my point.

Shiny sky's smiles

The unethically order of behaviour where fate begins to unravel inside an unmeasurable dialogue within earth. The rain on the plains don't shine from underneath the graze. It came from the sky and shine down onto your smile.

As Life's in an image

The window's in a frame

The heart's in a cage

The dog's in a kennel

Your feet are nowhere to be found

The parrots still talking to himself

Who's a pretty birdy "croak"

The cat's never at home

I feel the tears

I shine the brass

I kiss the bridle

I hear the wobble I slice the cake

I dip the cherry I break the glass I kindle my other half

Who touched my arse? Who feels the pain?

I threw the roses

We walk away even more far apart

for the wrong choices

Poem Poam

The truth behind the game,

Espionage is too deep for words too deep for mimics

and too deep for quotes,

This game is played with a total denial of indoctrination.

Poem Poam

Spoil them with youth

Forever lasting friendships

Love dives beyond doubt

While time belongs to itself

only if there's essence.

The incompetents of time is

the micro mystery.

Or to best friend of you legendary intense,

Catastrophe.

Poem Poam

To hell for less than another day or something bitter than a better tomorrow, I'll be already dead by then.

The, Evil of equident was only a business matter. With emotional consequences from deviants and laws of court rulings which upheld the devolution.

Poem Poam

Finding a impossible cure,

Is like unwinding an impossible curse.

Unwinding an impossible curse is like

Finding an impossible cure,

To cure for bananas syndrome,

Is like finding a cure for the size of an elephant's brain.

Which is only, A mystical metaphor of interest from the inevitable impacts of impossibilities.

Poem Poam

Life in a question

Life is not, A job

Life is, A dictatorship

Even if your without a job

You will be cantered by your own mistakes

You will take control of your own decisions

But who will depend upon your destiny

The world is at stake your world

Poem Poam

What's life

Without means

What's wrong

Without right

Love me without

Conditional stereo

Types

Just love

Me

Only

One

Second

Will

Change

Your

Lifetime

Forevermore.

Poem Poam

I possess the poison

I lose my mind

I fear control

The indoctrination of black people still persists

Poem Poam

Crows in a distance

Locusts swarm

Heavenly meteor

I peck for worms

Rigidly early hours of the morn

Desert landscape felt swiftly

Suddenly winds gobbles down my neck

My worms then to a mince.

Poem Poam

I walk the walls towards the golden gate of darkness

For the tribes of justice

Giving me the pace to stay alive threw the harshness

I ate plenty of pigeon along the way

No food no hunger wasn't the way

When I reached my demised

I swallowed flies as well

But who cares there be diseases everywhere

The ghost of the walls were speaking back to me through every angle of the way

I tried to leave the winds behind me

I felt a tap upon my shoulder I looked over

"But" Nobody was there I started running

Trap trap, they be surrounding me everywhere

Poem Poam

To every question

There's an answer

To where every

prophecy there's

A tale

The hit fall memories

Of

J.F.K

Tupac

&

Malcom X

Will never be found

Not to be forgotten

THE END